Just Dance

Hip-Hop Dance

Wendy Hinote Lanier
and Madeline Nixon

www.av2books.com

Step 1
Go to **www.av2books.com**

Step 2
Enter this unique code

KUNJDXWJU

Step 3
Explore your interactive eBook!

AV2 is optimized for use on any device

Your interactive eBook comes with...

Contents
Browse a live contents page to easily navigate through resources

Audio
Listen to sections of the book read aloud

Videos
Watch informative video clips

Weblinks
Gain additional information for research

Try This!
Complete activities and hands-on experiments

Key Words
Study vocabulary, and complete a matching word activity

Quizzes
Test your knowledge

Slideshows
View images and captions

...and much, much more!

Hip-Hop Dance

Contents

Hip-hop dancers are known for their fun, energetic styles.

Chapter 1

What is Hip-Hop Dance?

The street party begins. It is time to dance. Hip-hop is an athletic style of street dance. Dancers might pop or lock. They might spin on their heads or backs. Break dancing moves are common, too.

Hip-hop dance is part of hip-hop **culture**. The culture includes music and art, too. Hip-hop began in the 1970s. It started in the Bronx in New York City. Neighborhoods there hosted block parties. Usually, a **DJ** hosted the event. Clive Campbell was one of them. He and his sister hosted a block party in the summer of 1973. Their goal was to raise money to buy new school clothes.

Dance Tip

You need good upper-body strength to break-dance. Increase upper-body strength by doing push-ups or working with a weighted ball.

Clive Campbell's nickname is DJ Kool Herc.

Breaking is often done in groups.

Clive was only 16 years old. But his style caught on. Clive began **isolating** drum breaks in popular music. This involved two **turntables**. He switched back and forth between them. These breaks could be repeated. This gave dancers plenty of time to show off their moves.

DJ Kool Herc's party was held at **1520 SEDGWICK AVENUE** in the Bronx on **AUGUST 11, 1973**.

Clive's party was the birth of hip-hop. Clive was the first to call the dancers break boys and break girls, or b-boys and b-girls. Their style of dancing soon became known as breaking, or break dancing.

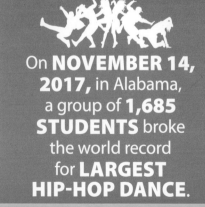

On **NOVEMBER 14, 2017,** in Alabama, a group of **1,685 STUDENTS** broke the world record for **LARGEST HIP-HOP DANCE**.

Hip-Hop Timeline

Hip-hop has changed and expanded over the years. It has gone from dance local to neighborhoods in New York City, to appearing worldwide. Film and theater contributed to the spread of hip-hop outside of the United States. Now, there are competitions, dance groups, and music across the globe.

1973

DJ Kool Herc throws the first hip-hop party.

1973-1976

Hip-hop group The Lockers appear on *The Tonight Show*, *Soul Train*, *Saturday Night Live*, and *The Dick Van Dyke Show*. Their appearances spread dance moves such as breaking, popping, and locking across the United States.

1981

The Lincoln Center for the Performing Arts hosts a break dancing battle between two hip-hop groups, the Dynamic Rockers and the Rock Steady Crew. Articles in *The Daily News* and *National Geographic* appeared after this event, giving hip-hop more visibility.

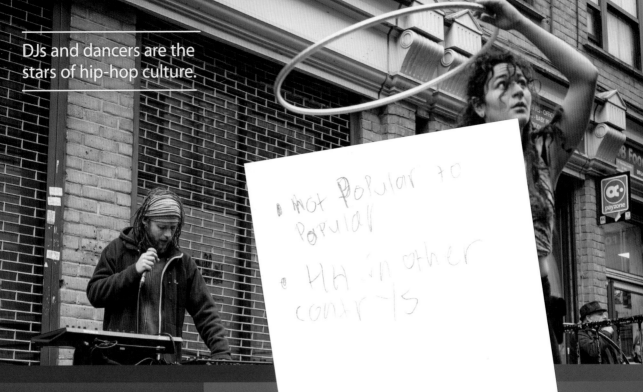

DJs and dancers are the stars of hip-hop culture.

Handwritten note (on sticky note):
- Not Popular to Popular
- HH in other countrys

1982–1983

Hip-hop begins to appear in films, such as *Wild Style and Flashdance,* once more showing how widespread hip-hop has become.

The Rock Steady Crew dances for Queen Elizabeth II, introducing hip-hop to European audiences.

Today

Hip-Hop is still extremely popular. *Hamilton*, the 2015 Broadway musical, won multiple Tony Awards for the use of hip-hop in song and dance.

Chapter 2

What to Wear

Hip-hop dancers create their own style. Clothes usually reflect **urban** street wear. Many dancers wear sweatpants or cargo pants. Oversized T-shirts or hoodies are common. Others prefer tank tops.

Hip-hop costumes often reflect their street-wear roots.

The key is to dress in layers. Layers are removed to cool off when needed.

Busting a big move can be dangerous. Safety gear helps prevent injuries. Dancers sometimes wear wrist pads, elbow pads, and knee pads.

Sneakers or soft-soled shoes work great for hip-hop. High-top sneakers are a popular choice, too. For **competitions** or **exhibitions**, some people have a special pair.

Hip-hop dancers dress to look good and move freely.

Dance Tip

Dance shoes should allow the dancer to slip and spin. If the soles grip too hard, dancers can fall or injure themselves.

Hip-hop dancers combine many different types of movements.

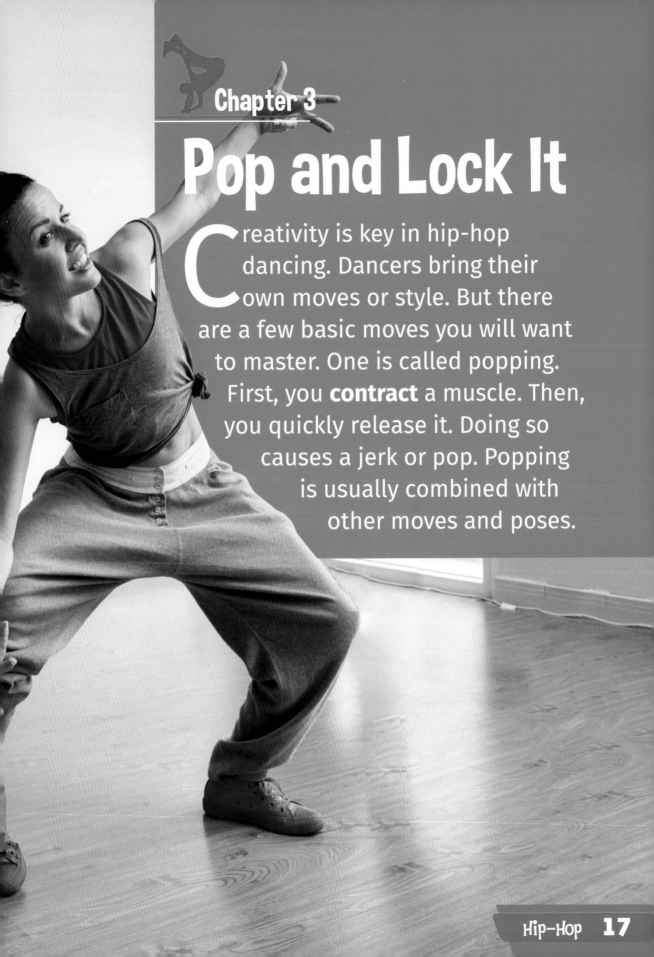

Chapter 3

Pop and Lock It

Creativity is key in hip-hop dancing. Dancers bring their own moves or style. But there are a few basic moves you will want to master. One is called popping. First, you **contract** a muscle. Then, you quickly release it. Doing so causes a jerk or pop. Popping is usually combined with other moves and poses.

Locking is also common. It starts when a dancer makes a quick move. Then, the dancer locks into position for a few seconds. Locking is often done to make viewers laugh.

The boogaloo is another basic move. It uses mostly the hips and legs. Dancers try to make it appear as if they have no bones.

Breaking is one of the best-known parts of hip-hop dance. It features fun, **acrobatic** moves. Head spins are common. So are back spins.

Break dancers often use their hands in their moves.

HH moves jazz and funk

Head spins are a break dancing move that always impress the crowd.

Some moves are unique to hip-hop dance. Hip-hop dancers also borrow moves from other **social** dances. They might use jazz or funk moves. Sometimes, they even look to gymnastics or martial arts. These moves are combined with basic hip-hop **choreography**. This is often seen in music videos.

Dance Tip

Watch other dancers to find fresh ideas. You can try to copy their moves.

The Cradle

Any good dance needs a killer ending. A freeze move called the cradle does the trick.

1. Start by sitting with your feet tucked under your bottom. Your knees should be spread apart.

2. Press your arms together. They should touch from the wrist to the elbow.

3. Keep your elbows firmly against your stomach. Lean forward. Open your arms and place your hands on the floor.

4. Now lift yourself up onto your hands. Turn your head to the side. Now freeze!

High-energy moves make hip-hop dance fun to watch.

Chapter 4

Show Off with Your Crew

By the 1980s, hip-hop dance was becoming popular. It was featured in movies. Some television shows had hip-hop dancers, too. And the style continued to gain popularity. By the 1990s, hip-hop dance was in many music videos.

Today's hip-hop dancers often perform without a set plan. They can be creative. This is called hip-hop freestyling. It includes classic hip-hop moves. But the best freestyling includes some original moves, too.

Dance groups are called crews. Sometimes, they challenge each other to friendly competitions. The competitions are called battles.

Dance battles allow dancers to show off their best moves. Freestyling, dance crews, and battles are the main ingredients of the hip-hop style.

Break dancers must be strong to show off their most acrobatic moves.

Hip-hop competitions can be more than just neighborhood dance-offs.

Competitions are held all over the world. Some are featured on TV. They give dance crews a chance to win money and recognition. Judges look for creative routines and flawless moves. They give each crew a score. A 10 is a perfect score.

Hip-hop dance is a great way to have fun and make new friends. And with a little practice, you could bust a move with the best of them.

In **1983**, Michael Jackson popularized the **MOONWALK**, also known as the hip-hop move, the **BACKSLIDE**, while performing his song, **BILLIE JEAN**.

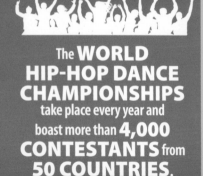

The **WORLD HIP-HOP DANCE CHAMPIONSHIPS** take place every year and boast more than **4,000 CONTESTANTS** from **50 COUNTRIES**.

Hip-hop crews practice hard to make sure their moves hit hard and correctly in competition.

Quiz

1 How does the boogaloo make dancers appear?

2 Who popularized the moonwalk, or backslide?

3 Who helped start hip-hop dance?

4 What is a perfect score at a competition?

5 What dance styles does hip-hop borrow moves from?

6 Why is locking done?

7 What is the key in hip-hop dancing?

8 Where did hip-hop originate?

9 What did Clive Campbell call boys and girls who were break dancing?

10 Which Tony Award winning musical features hip-hop dances?

Key Words

acrobatic showing skillful control of one's body

choreography the arrangement of steps and movements for a dance

competitions events in which teams try to beat each other

contract to bring a muscle together and make it shorter

culture beliefs, customs, art, and social interactions of a certain group of people

DJ a person who plays music for dances and parties

exhibitions displays or demonstrations for the public

isolating setting something apart from the rest

social having to do with activities involving other people

turntables machines that spin records

urban relating to a city environment

Index

Get the best of both worlds.

AV2 bridges the gap between print and digital.

The expandable resources toolbar enables quick access to content including **videos**, **audio**, **activities**, **weblinks**, **slideshows**, **quizzes**, and **key words**.

Animated videos make static images come alive.

Resource icons on each page help readers to further **explore key concepts**.

Published by AV2
350 5th Avenue, 59th Floor
New York, NY   10118
Website: www.av2books.com

Library of Congress Cataloging-in-Publication Data
Names: Lanier, Wendy Hinote, author.
Title: Hip-hop dance / Wendy Hinote Lanier and Madeline Nixon.
Description: New York, NY : AV2, 2021. | Series: Just dance | Includes
   index. | Audience: Ages 8-12 | Audience: Grades 4-6
Identifiers: LCCN 2019058807 (print) | LCCN 2019058808 (ebook) |
   ISBN 9781791123246 (library binding) | ISBN 9781791123253 (paperback) |
   ISBN 9781791123260 | ISBN 9781791123277
Subjects: LCSH: Hip-hop dance--Juvenile literature.
Classification: LCC GV1796.H57 L36 2021 (print) | LCC GV1796.H57 (ebook)
   | DDC 793.3--dc23
LC record available at https://lccn.loc.gov/2019058807
LC ebook record available at https://lccn.loc.gov/2019058808

Printed in Guangzhou, China
1 2 3 4 5 6 7 8 9 0   24 23 22 21 20

022020
101319

Project Coordinator: Heather Kissock   Designer: Ana María Vidal

Every reasonable effort has been made to trace ownership and to obtain permission to reprint copyright material. The publishers would be pleased to have any errors or omissions brought to their attention so that they may be corrected in subsequent printings.

Weigl acknowledges Getty Images, Alamy, iStock, and Shutterstock as its primary image suppliers for this title.

First published by North Star Editions in 2018.